Traveling Through

Selected Poems and Reflections

Revised Edition

William Yager

Zeta Publishing

Ocala, FL

Copyright © 2016, 2017 William Yager

All rights reserved. No part of this publication may be reproduced, distributed, or transmitted in any form or by any means, including photocopying, recording, or other electronic or mechanical methods, without the prior written permission of the publisher, except in the case of brief quotations embodied in critical reviews and certain other noncommercial uses permitted by copyright law. For permission requests, write to the publisher, addressed "Attention: Permissions Coordinator," at the address below.

Zeta Publishing, Inc
3850 SE 58th Ave
Ocala, FL 34480
www.zetapublishing.com

Ordering Information:
Quantity sales. Special discounts are available on quantity purchases by corporations, associations, and others. For details, contact the publisher at the address above.
Orders by U.S. trade bookstores and wholesalers. Please contact Zeta Publishing: Tel: (352) 694-2553; Fax: (352) 694-1791 or visit www.zetapublishing.com

First published by Xlibris in 2016

Rev. Date: 08/2017

ISBN: 978-1-947191-26-6 (sc)

ISBN: 978-1-947191-27-3 (e)

Library of Congress Control Number: 2017952562

Printed in the United States of America

Contents

Dedication..ix
Preface...xi
Odysseys' End...1
Christmas Gift...4
Tribute...7
Evening..8
Breath..9
The Pond..10
Blood Money...11
Big Lagoon..15
At Titlow Beach...16
Confident Crow...17
Calliope Song..19
Gift..20
A Name..22
Allium...23
Choice..24
Autumn...26
Belonging..27
Fog..28
September Musing..29
Fall..30
Going Home...31
On the Patio...33
Gifted...34
Grounded...35

Creeper	36
Impact	37
In The Garden	38
Boundaries	40
Spring Recital	46
Irony	47
Green	49
Emergence	51
Commodity	52
Seventeen Crows	53
Morning Grass	54
Meadow	55
Palisades	56
On Chambers Bay	57
Thank You	58
Poppy	59
Pneuma	60
Violet	61
Spring Morning	62
Soos Creek Pond	63
Psalm	64
Life	65
High	66
Relevance	67
Scotland Sunset	68
First Lily	70
EVA	71
Sun	72
The Leper's Bell	73
Last Lilies	76

Expressing	77
Where	78
Uniqueness	79
Snow	80
Surf	81
The Rose	82
Spent	83
The Birdbath	84
Reckless	85
Scent	86
Wednesday Morning	87
Offering	88
Surveillance	89
Seaside Reflection	90
Red	92
Grey	93
Tradition	94
What If	95
Inimitable	97
Reach	98
Tree Top Barber Shop	99
Thornrose	101
Material	103
The Journey	104
Time Out	105
Rhododendron	106
Shoreline Senses	107
Unless a Seed Falls	108
Valentine	110
Waves	112

Yellow	113
Without a Sound	114
Parabola	115
Trillium Gift	116
Riverbank Perspective	117
Rest	119
Soos Creek Closing	120
About the Author	121

Dedication

For Pat, beloved supporter, encourager without peer.

Preface

For most of my adult life I have been writing down my thoughts and reflections emerging from life around me, especially the beauty and wonder in Nature and that miraculous God-given process that envelops all of us. I have always maintained that these were "Notes to Myself", intended only to help structure and clarify my own thinking. But now in the sunset years of my life, I have been convinced to share these "Notes" with others.

There are some very special times when words make music and have rhythm. Sometimes insights and concepts come clearer in a new and different and unexpected context. A hummingbird's hovering, movement of the sun to catch a blossom just so, a leaf fluttering to the ground. At these distinctive moments, it seems that there is a metaphorical message, maybe even truth, buried within common surroundings and experiences waiting to be set free. I hope always to be an instrument in that release.

Odyssessys' End

At water's edge,
I cup my hand
and fill my palm,
all senses on high alert.

Numbingly cold
and crystal clear,
enough to sustain
life for a while.

And yet in the sameness
there must be illusion,
uniqueness beyond
what I see.

Miscible droplets
who each tell a tale,
odysseys confluent
in my curious hand.

Uniqueness in sameness,
a sojourner's journey
of global proportions,
choosing a wayside before me.
Down through the cold clarity,
the palm-reader's lifeline,

intertwined pathways,
a trek to my hand.

A bruising descent
down Victoria Falls,
Zambezi course
to the Indian Ocean.

Or northward bound
down the ancient Nile,
Egyptian oars
to enable.

Through Venezuelan jungles,
in Orinoco flow,
hosting life, giving life,
and Caribbean bound.

From the mighty Mississippi
to the Gulf of Mexico,
among the oily barges
and tankers do you flow.

From Himalayan highlands,
icy rooftop of the world,
were you then spewn
to Bengal Bay
by Ganges' overflow?
Or from Tibet's remote plateau,
the Mother of Waters flowed,

meandering Mekong made its way
to join South China's Sea.

Or down the great Yangtze,
seeking the sun,
you made your run
through shadowy canyons
etched with the tow-paths
of how many steps
treading their way
to the diligent docks of Shanghai.

Or were you a part
of the graceful blue Danube,
making your way to
the Blackest of Seas?

From Antarctic glaciers,
flanked by humpbacks and orcas,
you found Puget Sound
and the sand at my feet.

So here in my palm
full of spellbinding droplets,
each with a story to tell.
I think I'll sit down and listen.

William Yager

Christmas Gift

Joy to the world...
The Lord is come...
Emmanuel...
He is with us, and so we celebrate –
but *how* do we celebrate,
and *what* exactly are we celebrating?

As shoppers line up
as early as midnight,
Black Friday's the earliest gift.
Retailers celebrate
the shear possibility
that they might even be in the black
after this make-or-break
Christmas season.

Chinese manufacturers
are certainly celebrating
the glut that they've been
producing since summer.
Chinese girls at long tables
are painting, assembling, packing
they know not what or care,
but they will be able
to send home a few Yuan,
and so they're celebrating, too.

Though you'd never know to look at them.

Longshoremen unloading containers,
more than anyone ever has seen,
celebrating the fact
that they have a job
and might just be able to
buy some of the stuff
in these huge steel boxes from over the horizon.

The stocker at Wal-Mart
filling shelves through the night,
grateful to be called in for Christmas.
Everything seems more expensive this year,
and the kids wouldn't understand,
not only that Dad's not coming,
but maybe Santa, too.

Unsold trees in the parking lot
are beginning to drop their needles.
Thin green tears
mourning the end of another Season,
and what it was...
Joy to the world?

And yet...
The extravagant Creator
who started all this,
reaches through all the rubbish and trash,
ignorance and rejection,

somehow to love us anyway...
not because of anything *we* do,
but because of who *He* is.

How can this possibly be?
Look at what we have done:
to the gift-planet,
to each other,
to Jesus...
And what we have done to this celebration
makes all the Temple money-changers look like
saints...

And yet...
This Christmas season
we all can be heartened
by the clear revelation
that He can take it,
and that He forgives it and us.
And the incredible Gift of Himself
we see in Jesus,
not only *remains*,
but *transcends* anything we could do.
All the garishness, all the noise,
and all the irrelevance
cannot overwhelm the Still Small Voice...

Joy to the world... The Lord is come...

Tribute

Sentinels at attention
guarding the coastline,
black timbers reach for the sun.
Creosote undercoat
barnacle whitewash,
now host to the seagulls
and sleek fishing cormorants.

Patterned support posts
for an imposing structure
now gone unremembered,
but a critical conduit then.

Before there were bridges
to cross over the Narrows,
you might have docked ferries,
unloading, reloading
throughout the day.

Schedules and timetables
once governed your life;
now your fine-feathered guests
come and go as they please.

Evening

The evening sun
caressing the treetops
like a farewell embrace
until morning.

I know that the Earth
is the one that moves,
but the setting sun
is a majestic encounter.

The breath of God

In silence borne

moves the rose.

May that gentle Spirit

move me, too.

The Pond

Lily pads cover the pond,
as white blossoms soak in the sun.
Dark water seems to suspend them,
belying their roots in the mud.

But it's the nourishing
soil of our past
that has taught us,
shaped us,
enabled us,
inspired us,
to be what we are.

Our blossoms, too,
take in the sun and the rain,
the joy and the pain,
as we look to
the Source of it all.

Blood Money

Again it's the force of current events
that prompts the need for fresh thinking.
The Slaughter of Innocents haunts us today,
from Newtown, Connecticut,
this time,
as though the specter of Herod
were with us this Christmas, too.

As after each horrific tragedy,
the debate arises, again,
if ever so briefly:
why do we need so many guns?
assault weapons in the closet?
what are we so afraid of?

Consuming a diet of violence
as entertainment,
training young men to kill
with impunity in distant lands
and when they come back
wondering why

they don't instantly
reset to "normal".

The debate will rage
until the last child is buried,
and then the sage Congress
will feel the breeze of cash
cooling things off.

A serious look at
what's become of society
is clearly too hot to handle,
and certainly not the fare
of the re-electable.
It must be someone else's business:
maybe the churches need to step up,
since most parents abandoned
their charge long ago.
Besides, do we want
more Big-Brother government
telling us we don't need
a twenty-shot clip?
and assault rifles to shred
our targets of choice?

In the present hand-wringing time,
wrenching time of deep angst,
envisioning the small
bullet-riddled bodies
of innocent six-year-old children,
it all cries out for some kind of justice.
In our tear-filtered anguish,
what can we make of all this?

When it suits the purpose
of Powers That Be,
the emphasis on literalness
can be a great ally,
useful certainty and justification.
The Second Amendment
actually spells it all out,
outlines the right of a state to have
a "well regulated militia"
for its security from all the outsiders,
and therefore the right of the people
to "keep and bear arms".

Of course, in the eighteenth-century
the highest-technology
"arms" were single-shot,

muzzle-loading muskets.
Yet, does anyone think,
as he carefully wrote,
that even the great
Thomas Jefferson
could imagine an AK-47?

Gun runners and makers
and red politicians
marketing fear to suit
their own needs.
The boogey-man lurks
in various breeds,
from under the bed
or across the border.
In whatever form,
an alchemists dream,
turning lead into gold.

Big Lagoon

Sitting on the bluff at Big Lagoon:

solitude in September sun;

salty air and rhythmic ocean moaning.

Is it my yearning or

the evening rush-hour traffic?

At Titlow Beach

Waves lapping to the gravelly shore,

sea gulls' shoreline call,

saltwater airborne fragrance,

warming sun,

cooling breeze,

Narrows bridges' distant crossing,

the rumble of a sea-bound boat.

And time.

Confident Crow

As a child of God,
the confident crow
need not trust the bough
as it bends low
beneath her weight.

What is seen - the bending branch -
may or may not hold her at all.
But what is unseen,
that she knows from her birth,
is that she can fly…

Over-reliance on the
branches we see
displaces the power
within us to fly…

Seeing the unseen,
from blindness to sight,
from phantom strength
to genuine weakness,
from illusory independence
to total submission…

The root of our blindness,
the deception of Self,

leads us to think
we can do it...

But yielding our "freedom"
in exchange for submission?
Free slaves by choice
in the bosom of Love.

That must have been
what Jesus meant
when anointed he came
to give sight to the blind
and release for the captives -
even to Self.

Calliope Song

Mute Calliope,

geranium gift in crimson,

wakened by morning light,

obscuring clouds blown aside.

Caressed by the sun,

curtain going up.

Baton poised,

concert in scarlet.

Calliope's radiant song

inspiring my day.

The Gift

Trillium bloom in the heart of the forest:

intricate, delicate beauty on offer,

no thought of reward or compensation,

incomparable gift,

no conditions required,

no obligation implied.

If able to live,

it gives.

Giving and living are utterly inseparable.

All out, full throttle, nothing held back.

Total.

Motivation for giving is oxymoronic –

no motive at all is at hand,

giving the sole purpose for living.

The two so intimately entwined

as to be indivisible, fused.

Only one consuming purpose:

give.

Nothing more, nothing less,

no conditions…

Insight in the "grass of the fields"

seems to elude the foolishness

we humans call wisdom.

In perhaps the greatest

paradox of creation,

we, who have received so much more,

remain inclined to give so much less…

A Name

"Rufus-sided Towhee".

A ponderous moniker

for such a beautiful little bird,

hopping along in the midst of its life,

oblivious to its man-made label.

Maybe there's a time when

what we don't know is a blessing.

Allium pendulum

right side up

timeless purple gift

from Nature's clock.

The Choice

Come, as you must, to a fork in the road:
which way to go, and how will you choose?
The Knowing would say
it's of Culture or Christ.
(Can't there ever be more than two ways?)
Jesus said that the narrow road
is the one that leads to Life.
But the narrow way is obscured to us now
by the garish flashing neon sign:
"DETOUR! This is the way for Needful Things."
Broad, smooth and easy,
an autobahn of acquiescence,
minimum speed signs strictly enforced,
Culture-Police on high alert,
faster, faster, faster, faster.
No Different Drummer discernible here,
the dumbing-down process complete;
no time to think, should a remnant remain.
Only the Siren call up ahead:
winsome, seductive, destructive.

But the road crew's repairing the narrow way,
dismantling the Detour deception;
clearing the brambles of idols and theories,
filling the pot-holes and painting the fog-line,
progressive new thinking emerging at last.

And the narrow way lives up to its billing,
twisting and turning and climbing and falling,
delivering incomparable vistas:
revelations exposing Prodigal Love at each bend.
But the greatest discovery of all on the Way
is feeling the Road Builder's hand
and hearing His voice in each piece of creation,
"I always love you, just as you are…"

Autumn

Fall's full splendor
envelops me now,
like a fragrant, warm,
invisible blanket.
Phlox and sweet pea
yield their perfume
as a final hurrah.
The last lily blossom,
in a graceful adieu,
clings to the end
of its season,
giving completely
its final color
and fragrance.

Belonging

Sitting among the purple poppies,

looking out at blue hydrangeas,

the white of lilies and daisies,

and lavender lactifloras,

I feel a part of His growing creation.

Fog

The fog is moving
among the trees this morning,
covering imperfections and
quietly healing wounds,
like the Spirit of God
touching creatures of Earth.

Then slowly, gently -
the Sun,
heralded by intensifying light
celestial changing of the guard,
to embrace the woodland
with warmth and energy,
the hope of another new day.

The trees and I do our best to respond.
We remember the storms,
the cutting wind,
the culling caresses,
as we were thinned and trimmed
to grow straighter and stronger… later.

We remember sinking our roots
deeply into the nurturing moisture and
loam of our past, and
we hang on -
Greeting a new dawn, the fog, the sun,
and hope.

September Musing

Another leaf let go and fell,

leaving countless siblings behind,

a harbinger of fall, I'm afraid.

As yet, though, the greens prevail;

infinite shades to us fellow creatures .

Perhaps God has counted them.

Fall

Red-amber rain,

    spiraling,

        floating,

            coming to rest

                on the forest
    floor.

Maybe that's why

it's called "fall".

Going Home

The trek from East of Eden lay before me.
Mountains of Pride to scale and bring down,
self-sufficiency masquerading
as God-given talent to steward.

Sirens from rocks of Judgment await,
the sweet-sounding lure of Assessment,
vision obscured by the roiling sea
of Culture's mindless cacophony.

Deserts of blistering humility to cross,
occasional oases of insight.
Baptismal water and Eucharistic feast,
refreshing recollection of whose I am.

Awash in a world of identity theft,
bombarded by crass diminution,
saved by the life-ring of scriptural perception,
"transcending mind" hard at work.

"OK-ness" is not a hot seller:
we must be saved from being too fat
and looking too old is a downer.
Psst: "Here for a price is the answer".

Doubting a fourth century creed is unspoken

and focus on Jesus too risky.
Water it down and surely they'll come;
somehow the show must go on...

Screwtape rubbing his hands in delight,
the master deceiver triumphant.
The Western Road seems littered and lost,
signposts pointing away in profusion.

Then amid the stumbling blocks he glides.
The gentle touch of his mangled hand,
the iridescent music of his voice:
"I know the Way... Come on!"

On The Patio

Silk Road lily,
journey concluded,
magenta and white,
trumpeting fragrance,
gracing my patio table.

Three dozen red rubrum
recurved in the morning,
hummingbird's banquet.
Both of us blessed by
resplendence on offer.

Gifted

Modest white sweet pea

in the midst of the lilies,

unpretentious voice

in the vibrant visual chorus.

Blessed by your fragrance,

a solo performance

is yours for the asking,

but humility trumps a display.

Beauty in harmony

as we all play our parts,

knowing our gifts,

bringing our best to the mission.

Grounded

Roman gifts of viaducts and arches
came at a very high price.
The Janus face of "civilization",
borne on the sword of the Pax Romana,
established the pattern we drown in today.

Clipping the wings of the young church of Jesus,
the Way rendered needless within the gold cage,
external options foregone.
Roman obsession with organization
co-opting diversity's richness.

Inside the cage, order established,
power to control all the "others".
What to believe
and who's in and who's out,
the Namesake's mission abandoned.
Who wants to be poor, when rich is so pleasing?
So the cage was expanded for a palace or two,
and Temple exclusion was once more in place.

Creeper

Having crept to the limbs

and the outlying branches,

draping in elegance,

eclipsing the Gardens of Babylon,

because you are here.

Unseen breeze from somewhere

to here,

caressing the tendrils of red and green;

rhythmic undulation ...

Nature's autumn dance.

Impact

The last snow leopard,

having retreated so high,

curls in a cave,

and takes her last breath.

In the Garden

Overhead, the SeaTac flight path;

alongside, the freeway I-5.

But inside,

the roar of distant thunder

and crashing ocean waves

claiming the beach of my mind.

Along my path

a geography of blossoms:

from China and Burma,

Tibet and Japan,

they traveled here

to saturate my senses.

Rhododendron Rose

from the slopes of Yunan

to the receptive

soil at my feet,

they've come undeterred
to do what they know
wherever they grow:
to give in profusion.

What is He telling me,
extravagant God
of flowers and trees
and lavish bouquets?
Luxuriant creation
in all its abundance,
in all its exquisite detail,
in all its dependency,
includes even me.

Boundaries

New Year's Eve.
A new beginning?
The past is still with us
in one form or other,
and the future is still to unfold.

So what more have we done
than create an excuse
for yet another football game?

Bowls proliferate
as far and as deep
as television dollars extend.
And a whole distinct structure
of pseudo-competition
is fabricated to grow up
around the new money.
And overly serious
now player-experts
spew out the football-speak
as though it mattered.

On the next day, though,
another boundary is formed
between winning and losing

and consequent rankings,
with accompanying drivel-analysis.

Boundaries exist
between coaches as well:
those still employed and
those who are not.
It probably matters to them.

But entertainment per se
has always existed
to take us away
from where we find ourselves today.
From Punch and Judy
to some Taco Bowl,
we transcend Reality
and the fantasy border it names.

Of course, real boundaries
abound, as well.
But even where there
are natural margins,
there often is fuzziness
between one and the other,
especially in the
midst of two nations.

Even with life and death.
Is life in a heartbeat,

a pulse or a brain wave,
and death moving into their vacuum?
Or is life a matter of giving?
or loving?

Words, and even the
sentiment behind them,
certainly render new boundaries.
"I do" makes a statement
transforming who's single
to married,
committed, together,
formerly two and now one.

"Want to come?" is a bridge
from outside to inside,
excluded to included,
alone to together.
One of Them becomes
one of Us.
A path from anxiety
to peace in belonging.

Cultures too have layered
zones of personal comfort,
like invisible cocoons
surrounding a person,
delineating distance
for a range of exchanges.

Rivers and mountains and
deserts form boundaries
responding to natural
creative forces.
Obstacles in crossing
from one side to the other
could insulate groups
and provide co-existence
for a time.

Ambitious leaders
could change all that.
When Julius Caesar
crossed over the Rubicon,
he created an empire,
synonymous now
with a one-way filter,
a border with no going back.

Other boundaries are
socially created
to determine who's in and who's out;
who's with us, who's against us;
the haves and have-nots,
who takes and who yields.

Tribal togetherness
forged for survival

has morphed into innumerable
forms and dimensions.
Families and neighborhoods,
cities and towns,
states and nations
and alliances among them
all form loyalties
that are deeply supportive,
and massively dangerous.

The One who transcends
all human boundaries
continues to call us back Home,
back to the Garden
where it all started
and how it was supposed
to continue through time.
The Love of God crossed
all of the boundaries,
breaching the margins,
piercing the limits,
beyond our capacity to grasp,
even now.

How could the unworthy
suddenly be worthy?
How could the excluded
become embraced,
even celebrated like

the younger Lost Son?
How could all of the
delineations,
so meticulously drawn,
and all of the hierarchies,
carefully constructed,
and all of the segments
traditions built up
over thousands of years
simply dissolve?
Where have all the boundaries gone?
Darkness confronted by Light
disappears.

Spring Recital

A hundred hydrangeas
joined in the chorus
singing their praises to God.
Brilliant blue blossoms and
heart-shaped green leaves
taking their place on the risers.
Water and time and
the season empowered,
and the springtime rehearsal's concluded.
Lights dim in the hall
as a cloud passes by.
Now harmonies heard in the silence
exquisitely beautiful tones
Creator-composer's
gift overwhelming.
Program note: the concert is free,
dress code a thing of the past,
and seats are reserved
for all who would come -
just as you are.

Irony

Squirrels descend the tree headfirst;

they want to see what's ahead,

not behind.

Claws in bark, a pathway up,

just as sure when coming back down.

How far ahead do they need to see?

As far as the nut

or to you or to me.

Of the nuts on offer

the crows take their share,

their share being all they can get,

and yet…

The choice of both is to co-exist,

confrontation not occurring to them,

or having occurred all those eons ago,

was discarded as destructive,
disrupting the flow.

So, what can we see now
by looking back,
"history" distorted by winners?
It must be dissected
so Truth can be told;
what can we really
learn from our past?

But looking around the emptied room,
the learners all seem to have fled.
As Truth takes the roll,
counting not one,
Culture's pyrrhic victory won.

Green

The word reduced to
near meaninglessness,
dwarfed by the myriad
shades and tones and textures
each leaf and blade
changing minute by minute
responding to wind and sun
but still bearing its name all the same.

Spring full upon us,
gusting winds and
weeping clouds and
growing all around.
Intricate blossoms,
breath-taking beauty
emerging from seed-specks,
with a bow of gratitude

to sun and soil and rain
and the creative grace of God.

It seems that people, too,
though by a common name,
seem as complex and changing
as the wind-blown leaves,
emerging, maturing, and dying,
nourishing the next generation.

But how does what we leave behind
feed those who follow?
Beyond mawkish eulogies,
what is there lasting and real?
A word, an idea,
a model to follow?
Maybe even a paradigm shift.

Emergence

Up from the dark and the damp,

up from the depth of the pot.

In space not too far,

only inches from bottom to top.

But in time,

from autumn to spring.

Each green spear

penetrating the air,

announces a floral

chorus to come.

Summer symphony

of color and fragrance and shape,

all playing their parts.

Silent heavenly harmony.

Commodity

Deaf to a different drummer
due to the din of
Commodified Culture,
all form an orderly line,
over here,
in front of the register.

You're worth what you spend;
if you're poor,
that's not much.
But, no worries,
"no credit, no problem",
we'll sign you up anyway,
tomorrow you learn what it cost,
too late.
"Good News" for the poor
was not to have more,
but acceptance we surely can't buy,
and love we can't ever earn.

Seventeen Crows

From Herald Crow
the call's gone out
and now they've come
from who knows where.

She's been sighted and
the Peanut Lady,
like a modern day Sower,
as regular as sunrise,
casts her bounty
over the piebald lawn.
And they come.

The squirrels have joined
the company of scroungers,
pausing to run off
and bury their treasures.

Our home is a refuge
from threatening
encroachment, with
breakfast thrown into the bargain.
We pray their wild instincts
prevail when we're gone.

Morning Grass

Dew-drop diamonds,

countless rainbow treasures

salt the lawn.

From ninety million miles,

then comes the call.

And they're gone.

Meadow

In the middle of the meadow,

I stop to soak in the sun.

The quiet I'm in

belies the nighttime

host I know you were.

Palisades

Rain coming down
heavily now;
fog moving in to the shore.
What was seen before
is still there - unseen.

Numberless shades
of gray conspire
to obscure, while
awaiting the sun
and revelation.

The whole sky seems
to move overhead.
The breeze around
my hooded head
belies the massive force above;
the breath of God at work.

Quiet patio,
dry after the rain.
Stereo fountains and
the voice of St. Francis de Sales
from the etching:
"Suffering is either
diverted, or allowed
with the strength to endure it."

On Chambers Bay

The wind gusts are strong enough
to rock the car and
continue to sweep
the remaining leaves
from their branches.

Hosts for the year,
as they budded, emerged,
promising lush greenness
in myriad shades and hues.

In the fullness of time
the yellow came,
amber not far behind.
Through autumn's peak
the reds burst forth
and dazzled us
with their brilliant gift.
And now they too
are being blown away.
Growing, then ripe, then gone.

Thank You

Lace cap hydrangea
cobalt blue brilliance
framed by leafy companions
and early evening sun.

Mustering words of gratitude
the best that I can do,
ridiculously inadequate,
in the midst of this magnificence.

And then the unmistakable
rhythmic sound comes,
a tear-filtered hummingbird
right in front of my face.

Radiant green back,
iridescent red throat,
hovering before me to say,
"You are welcome."

Poppy

Purple poppy

parchment petal,

translucent in early evening sun.

Twelve blossoms now

where yesterday

there was one.

Pneuma

Majestic firs,

green forest stalwarts,

yielding their crowns

to the breath of God.

Would that we

could so respond.

Violet

In early March it came,
seeking warmth and light
from the sun,
often disappointed in both.

But soldiering on,
beneath detection,
struggling up and on out,
green tendrils peeking
up over the edge
(a miniature periscope checking us out?).

Decision made,
it ventures forth,
choice-less choice to grow,
and then give.

Billions of years
and the history its logged,
the universe still home
to the violet and me.

Spring Morning

How many versions of Green can there be?

The Earth spins a second

and a thousand new variants are born

as sunlight and shadow dance in my wood.

Then high in their branches

the fir trees respond

to the unseen press of the breeze,

willing respondents

to the Spirit's persuasion.

In my verdant cathedral

from deep in my being

my prayers join the pillars

ascending to God.

Soos Creek Pond

Dragon flies dart

over dark pond stillness.

Glossy reflection,

broken by the

mallard gliding by.

Clusters of lily pads,

interrupted only

by the occasional

sun-seeking bloom.

Peace.

Psalm

Sanctuary spires,

treetops reflecting the sun,

together in green embrace.

Worship.

Interlocking pieces

in a thousand

thousand ways -

no puzzle box lid.

High

To be in the tree tops

two hundred feet in the air…

A dream for me, but

a daily routine for

the knowing crow.

Relevance

When the seat beside me

is taken by Him,

when the solid shoulder

gives me strength, or

when looking up ahead,

He beckons to me:

all the fear and

all the judgment and

all the creeds and

all the confessions and

all the inquisitions and

all the structures and

all the committees and

all the exclusions and

all the self-righteousness

are just mist…

Scotland Sunset

I gazed on the face of Loch Linnhe that night,
her cool deep reflection inviting me in,
to drown in the depths where no one can see,
a solace complete as that day.

But a low-flying eagle disrupted my thinking,
as God's intervention he bore.
With wings pressing down on the cool evening air,
straight to the heart of the darkness he flew.
And dropping one pebble,
he changed life forever,
as the hypnotic dark mirror he shattered.
A rippling reality, newly transformed,
flowed to the shore of my soul.

There's a mystical moment
'tween daytime and dusk,
in the silence of sunset
as twilight time stops.
As God of the Cosmos
pores over his ledgers,
comparing his plans with our own.

My wry-smiling Friend
placed his hand on my shoulder
and then said to me,

"Son, you're not done.
There is life yet to live
beyond all you imagined,
a mountain or two yet to climb.

There is love unexperienced,
both hers and my own,
to nurture, sustain you
as ascending you go.
I will not forsake you,
and give you this blessing:
Be peaceful, my children,
and know I am Love."

First Lily

Regal announcement

six-petaled trumpets

standing together

their time in the lime-light

as Stentorian silence

brings all to attention:

breath-taking splendor

of blossoms and fragrance.

Summer's begun.

Spider suspended

stepping on space

midair miracle and

mundane routine.

Sun

What was I doing
eight minutes ago
when the sun that I'm feeling
started traveling?

Rotation I know,
and orbits I get,
head-tripping along,
and yet...

It's gravity, I know,
that keeps me in place
as I hurtle through space,
and yet...

Around and around,
a thousand miles an hour,
a dizzying tempo,
and yet...

As the sun warms my back,
and I drink in the stillness,
refreshingly tranquil,
and yet...

Though knowing my movement,
while relishing quiet,
I'll move my chair
and follow the sun.

The Leper's Bell

Unclean warning...
the Clean to stay away.
Forlorn moaning...
ringing accompaniment,
a chorus of death from exclusion.

But the bell we hear now
concludes the day's trade,
of winners and losers,
of margins and money,
usurious deception,
oblivious to counting the cost.

Commodified culture
of spending, pretending.
The bell of repulsion
now rings with the Sirens:
winsome, alluring, wreckage complete.

Numbers and prices,
computer chips humming:
a ton of coal or
an ounce of face cream,
a bushel of corn or
designer blue jeans.
Did it come from Zimbabwe

or Mexican maquila
or dim Chinese sweatshop
or hot Bangladesh?

Young girls at long tables
twelve hours a day
painting the Christ child in April;
a room full of sew-ers
drenched in the din of
industrial machines
and the incessant flow
of more pieces.

Two millennia
and a world away,
the cry went out
on the dusty road
and the bells rang their warning,
Unclean!

But our three o'clock bell
closing trading day chaos,
applauding contagion disguised,
celebrates suicide's ringside seat.

"Good news for the poor"
is what Jesus brought,
but their numbers are growing
with each clang of the bell.
So the News must be larger

and louder than ever,
sweeter than the
well-disguised Sirens.

We need to ask questions:
How much is enough?
What is the cost of our choices?
Time for the Church to step up
to the challenge of Culture,
exposing the Decepter
and his hawking of
"Needful Things".

Who else will lead us?
Stop selling fear and
focus on Jesus
and the love of the Father
he showed us.
Lead us the Way
back to Eden…

Last Lilies

Elegant gift of white and scarlet,

highlighted by autumn sun,

caressed by the gentlest

afternoon breeze.

Could it be our

ubiquitous God,

disguised as a lily,

is teaching us to give

here and now?

Expressing

One freeway now

has added express lanes,

and emblazoned above,

the alluring advantage:

make the next city

two minutes earlier,

only 75 cents

for ten miles of the lane.

Now,

what shall we do

with the two minutes

we bought?

Where

A passenger jet flies overhead,
two or three hundred people aboard.
Friday evening,
and going somewhere
seeing someone at last.

Home for the weekend,
a trip overseas;
A wedding?
A funeral?
Vacation from school?
To hearth and home or
weekend in Vegas.
Who knows?

They don't know
I'm down here below them
and I don't know who they are
or where they're going -
or why.

But I see them up there
in that aluminum tube
sharing this moment
in space and time,
in a few hours dispersing.
Deeper connection
deferred for a while.

Uniqueness

Unique among creation's spawn

the human ego swims upstream,

knowing too much;

knowing too little.

Snow

Pristine covering,

superficial beauty,

but what is beneath

the mantle of purity?

Surf

Relentless
in its rise and fall,
the pounding surf comes at us.
And over time,
a shoreline life is crafted.

But this boundary we see
'tween water and land,
often delineates nations, as well,
no less than the shifting Sahara sands
or the Western winners in 1919.

A pencil line drawn,
describing a country,
but cutting a people in two.
Complex decisions
for sure in the making.
No one is happy,
but pleasing the powers that be
seems in order.

So, pensive at surfside
or thinking of current events,
the tide will come at us
and force us to be present.

William Yager

The Rose

Pink rose beacon

in a varied sea of green,

alone, but not lonely,

heaven-scent giving.

Spent

Grey-brown tendrils,

still,

in the windless autumn sun.

A season ago,

you were green and growing.

In the fall, now,

flamed out,

wanting only to sleep.

William Yager

I cleaned out the birdbath
and filled with clean water,
and it didn't take long
for the unwritten notice
to be broadcast abroad.

A non-descript sparrow,
exuding great joy,
washed and splashed
and then flew away…

So, why do we reach out
to them in this way,
so the birds will say,
"Thank you",
and make us feel good for our gift?

Or is filling the birdbath
in the nature of things
of just Giving…
The sparrow's reception
in taking her gift,
echoes the ease
of God's closer creatures
to bask in His absolute love.

Reckless

Infinite wisdom of freedom once given, risking rejection, enabling Love.

Scent

On the broad back

of the soft summer breeze

its fragrance is carried to me:

Eau de Sweet Pea.

Wednesday Morning

Beyond the trees

and blocks away

the rattle and groan

of the refuse truck

interrupts my tranquil world.

In its weekly routine

reaching out to grasp,

absorbing our trash,

taking away all our garbage:

the grace of God on wheels.

Offering

From all those millions of miles away,

the gift of as many rainbows.

All the colors in God's great creation

captured in countless dew drops

coming to adorn my morning.

Surveillance

Somewhere up in

the swaying branches,

unseen eyes look down.

What to make of one old guy

with a faded Hawks cap,

and a yellow pad and pen?

Friend or foe or food source?

We'll wait and see.

Maybe he's just dreaming.

Seaside Reflection

Waves lapping at mossy rocks,

carried ashore on the incoming tide.

Then,

responding to lunar persuasion,

you go.

Bidding adieu to

the barnacled beach

for the compelling beckon

of another shore;

how many continents away?

But sharing the language

of ebbing then flowing,

plunging to sea-depths unknown.

Do the rocks know where you've been,

or care?

Did you glide ashore

on a tropical beach

or wreak havoc on

Japanese coastlines?

With no obligation

except to respond:

gentleness or power,

formation, destruction.

All by-products of

forces outside.

Primeval orders obeyed.

Red

It wasn't there yesterday.

Yet high in the graceful tresses,

caressed by the

evening breeze,

it announces the

beginning of autumn:

the first red leaf.

Without clock or calendar,

the new season's herald

clings to its stem

for a few more hours,

and then lets go.

Grey

How many shades of grey

in a day without sun?

Bay water coming in on the tide,

Clouds drifting in on the wind,

no sun,

no shadow,

but no joy?

Tradition

A hawk has entered
the crow's domain
and even without
their eggs to protect,
the territorial intrusion
is intolerable:
he must go!

Conditioned by eons
of self-preservation,
fine points of the present
irrelevant, indeed.

So, how do we move
from the Past to the Present;
how do we deal with
conditions which formed us?
We cherish our Past
as a springboard to Now,
but a course to the Then
without question?

What If

What if Emperor Constantine
had left alone the People of the Way?
What if in their scatteredness
they sustained their focus on Jesus?

What if on their Way they went
without the bishops out front?
What if they eschewed
the Babel Tower
of doctrines and creeds
and conditions.

What if they declined
to be organized,
centralized,
doctrinized,
homogenized,

neutralized?

In the smothering structure and
inherent ranking,
dazzling jewels and
ring-kissing protocol,
where to find Jesus?

The founder evicted…
no room in the Inn,
once again.

Inimitable

Courageous tulip,

surrounded on all sides

by so many varied greens,

different in shape,

different in size,

destined to grow and encroach.

That the beacon of scarlet

was first in the patch

doesn't seem to matter to them.

Reach

I wonder if

within every soul

there is a rose.

And the God-like aspect

in each one of us

is to reach past

the thorns of the other,

to find the flower within.

Tree Top Barber Shop

Icy shampoo

amply applied with

rain in the deep freeze

that used to be

our back yard.

Then bang, bang, bang, bang!

(Fourth of July out of step.)

A whisper of wind-comb

lighting the fuses.

Too-burdened branches,

ice-laden treetops,

splintering firs,

all yielding to Earth's

irresistible call.

Miracles of
falling trees missing cars.
Chain-sawed path to the street.
Yet trees in their place
an answer to prayers.

Temperatures rising,
snow receding,
ice melting:
Nature's divine intervention.

Time for a deep breath,
tragedy averted.
Now for the chainsaw…
and the heating pad.

Thornrose

I hold the rose,
drawn down into its
delicate beauty,
awestruck by a miniature
of the life we've been given,
layered and subtle and
growing and dying.
Petaled profusion and
budding redemption.

I hold the rose,
inhaling its gift of
perfumed splendor
and with it
the fragrant breath of life.
Gift given for a time
in our rising and falling,
its celestial ribbon untied.

I hold the rose,
tightening my grip on its stem,
absorbing its mesmerizing
rainbow of color,
the pain of its thorns
cutting deeply endured,
the tender exchange gladly made.

From moment to moment
we hold life in our hands,
its beauty and fragrance
and nuance and pain.

We hold for an instant
the seeds of creation,
the growing and dying and
life come again.

In holding the rose
I'm holding the orchid
and nightshade, as well.
Pleasure and pain,
darkness and light,
beginnings and endings and
growth in between.

In holding the rose
I'm embracing the gift
of the Cosmos Creator
whose extravagant love
for this speck in His space
ignites my heart and
heals my wounded hand.

Material

A Carpenter's dream,

half a world away,

in foggy mountains

far removed

from the dusty plains

of Palestine.

But two millennia

of solar circuits

and here I am,

under a giant redwood tree.

The Journey

Up from the Earth,
out from the sea,
loving creation:
"Let there be…"

And we all responded,
(who could say no?)
to gentle persuasion
and chances to grow.

The conditions were perfect
(how else could it be?)
with the hand of the Master
setting us free.

Evolving together
traversing the ages,
myriad paths to this place:
crows and ants and fir trees and me.

Time Out

Tired of climbing,

tired of leafing,

tired from turning,

tired from shedding.

Time to hang bare

in the autumn sun;

time for a season of sleep.

Rhododendron

Deep in the forest,

lush rhododendron

giving its magnificent bloom,

never questioning

that no one else is there.

Shoreline Senses

Smelling the water,

watching the currents,

feeling the sun,

hearing the seagulls,

tasting the salt air:

drenched by the gifts of God.

Unless A Seed Falls

The miracle of spring...
of sun and rain and growth.
From dormant seeds and tubers and bulbs,
deep and damp and dark in soil,
yet with the germ of Life – waiting.

In his parable, perhaps
Jesus' powerful analogy
refers not just to himself,
but also to all of us.
To be born again
requires a death,
shucking off the old
to make room for the new to occur.

Paul wrote about
"living sacrifice",
not dead but reborn;
and this
from transforming our minds,
thinking in a new way,

being in a new way.

The seed not going
into the soil
stays just a seed,
foregone potential,
ironically, its death
by not dying.

But grasping our freedom
from ego-direction,
we transcend instinctual
self-preservation,
imbedded in life gone before,
and trade it for
perfect abundance.

Valentine

Not as twenty-somethings
did we come to what we have,
but as fifty-somethings,
starting new nonetheless.
Interlocking pieces
seeking ins and outs
to make a fit.
A promising new picture
emerged over time,
faded puzzle box covers long gone.

With children having children,
memories reconstituted
like some instant bouillon mix;
diapers, strollers, sleepless nights
come forward again,
an empathetic dream.

Like fine wine and cheddar cheese

(oh, please),

some would even risk

clichéd analogies,

trying to capture, describe

what to us is simply

warm, complicated, growing, alive…

So what do we have, after all,

in this late-season blending:

Heinz 58 times two?

Deepening understanding,

growing tolerance,

intense caring,

unwavering support…

Love.

Waves

Coming ashore
up the stony beach
one after another
after another.

But each one comes
successively further,
and further yet.
I wonder why?

After that they recede.
Each one lapping
the shore further out,
further out.

Then comes the signal
at some unknown point
and they turn again -
return journey
to the same stony shore.

I could examine this
mesmerizing pattern
for all the days I have left
and never once credit
Sister Moon.

Daffodil sentries
lining the path,
guarding the way,
as though for a
royal procession.
They didn't seem to care
that I was only
going to the shed
for my mower.

Without a Sound

Our squirrely friends,

they bound across

the pock-marked ground,

green and brown,

that used to be lawn.

Their subterranean cousins

have pushed up mounds,

putting artillery targets to shame.

Sharing a home,

above and below,

I wonder if they know each other?

Parabola

A red-orange leaf
has just come to rest,
free-falling down to my table.
All energy spent,
turning greens into red,
it must be tired
like me.
Time to call it a day
and a season.

Now you will nourish
the soil and the roots
that you came from.
Winter slumber
and time to replenish
the leafless brown stems
and the life that they nurture,
waiting.

Like a morning alarm
in the late springtime grayness,
reluctantly up and about,
the brown barren branches
have come to full term
and their latent leafing is ready.
A pregnant bulge then
greenish emergence;
a new season begun once again.

Trillium Gift

I looked into the woods
and a hundred feet away
a Trillium looked back at me:
silent, solitary, majestic.

From beneath the dark soil,
when the timing was right,
the green spear emerged,
a non-event
for the passing squirrel.

But for those who can see,
and for those who can feel,
consciousness opens
with the blossom,
and the silent Trillium
bellows the grace of God.

Riverbank Perspective

Standing on its south bank,
I am mesmerized
by the Puyallup River's flow,
strong, slow, determined,
westward bound to Commencement Bay,
moving inexorably
from my right to my left.

On the opposite north shore
my friend is enthralled
by the River's relentless run
from his left to his right.

We meet and are
respectively convinced
that it is moving from
right to left, and from left to right.
But how can it be both?
After all, seeing is believing…

Our conundrum is only resolved
when we shift our focus,
our frame of reference,

from ourselves to the River, itself.
Regardless of where we stand,
the River is determinedly
flowing westward.

So, perhaps in our quest
to understand God more fully,
we need to move further away
from what has been written
and preached and persuaded
over the centuries in the Tradition,
to what we think Jesus, himself,
said and did:
then, the angry, punishing God
of rules, sanctions and fear
becomes the God of Jesus,
of forgiveness, inclusion,
and incredible unbounded love…

Rest

Flowers get tired

and lie down,

like me.

Bright colors faded,

sweet fragrance gone.

Where?

I wonder...

William Yager

Soos Creek Closing

Pond lily blossoms
close up for the night.
Tomorrow's sun will
herald new beginnings.

The people are leaving,
happy talk fading,
soft silent breezes
filling the vacuum
their withdrawal leaves behind.

And I am quietly
embraced by the trees.
The evergreen next to me
seems to be nodding,
a dragon fly adding his gesture:
"until next time".

About the Author

William Yager experienced his early adolescent years in the midst of the redwood forests of northern California. In retrospect, his spiritual sensitivity and deep love of Nature took root during this time.

Following degrees in mechanical engineering from the University of California, Berkeley, and an MBA from the Harvard Business School, he was in systems engineering and management in the computer industry in San Francisco for fifteen years .

A year of reflection and reassessment resulted in making the transition to the Pacific Northwest, and a teaching career was launched at Whitworth College in Spokane, Washington. In 1984, Bill and his family moved to Eugene, Oregon, where he completed his Ph.D. at the University of Oregon in International Strategic Management.

Now retired after twenty years on the School of Business faculty at Pacific Lutheran University, he is able to appreciate all the more the profound God-given gifts in Nature and to indulge his love of reading and writing.

He and Pat have six adult children, nine grandchildren, and live in Tacoma, Washington.

www.ingramcontent.com/pod-product-compliance
Lightning Source LLC
Chambersburg PA
CBHW021153080526
44588CB00008B/323